ROCKS, MINERALS AND RESOURCES

Gold

Ron Edwards and James Gladstone

Crabtree Publishing Company
www.crabtreebooks.com

Crabtree Publishing Company

www.crabtreebooks.com

PMB 16A, 350 Fifth Avenue,
Suite 3308,
New York, NY 10118

612 Welland Avenue,
St. Catharines,
Ontario, Canada
L2M 5V6

73 Lime Walk,
Headington,
Oxford, 0X3 7AD
United Kingdom

Coordinating editor: Ellen Rodger
Contributing author: Rona Arato
Production coordinator: Rosie Gowsell
Design: Brad Colotelo, Rosie Gowsell
Copy editors: Sean Charlebois, Carrie Gleason
Production assistant: Samara Parent
Scanning technician: Arlene Arch-Wilson
Art director: Rob MacGregor
Photo research: Allison Napier
Prepress and printing: Worzalla Publishing Company
Consultants: Dr. Richard Cheel, Professor of Earth Sciences, Brock University
Project development: Focus Strategic Communications Inc.
Contributors: Ron Edwards and James Gladstone

Photographs: AP/Wide World Photos: p. 13 (top), p. 25 (top); Burke/Triolo/Getty Images p. 9 (bottom); Gerald Cubbit, p. 17 (top); Gianni Dagli Orti/CORBIS/MAGMA, p. 28; Robert Estall/CORBIS/MAGMA, p. 30 (top right); Robert Garvey/CORBIS/MAGMA p. 20; Raymond Gehman /CORBIS/MAGMA, p. 17 (bottom); Kevin Jordan, Getty Images, p. 30 (bottom); Layne Kennedy/CORBIS/MAGMA, p.15; Araldo de Luca/CORBIS/MAGMA p.10 (bottom); John Madere/CORBIS/MAGMA p.31 (bottom left); Fernando Moleres/Panos, p. 19 (bottom right); Charles O'Rear/CORBIS/MAGMA, p. 14; Mark Peterson/CORBIS/MAGMA, p. 26 (top); Siede Preis/Getty Images, p. 15 (top right); Carmen Redondo/CORBIS/MAGMA,

title page; Karen Robinson/Panos, p. 26, bottom; Paul A. Souders/CORBIS/MAGMA, p. 22; Janet Wishnetsky/CORBIS/MAGMA, p.29 (right); Chris Shinn/Mira.com, p. 6 (right); Bettman/CORBIS/MAGMA, p. 27, 31; Birmingham Museums and Art Gallery/Bridgeman.co.uk, p. 24; Digital Vision/Getty Images, gold coin images, title page; Getty Images, p.10 (top right); Hulton Archive by Getty Images, p. 9 (left), 7, 11, 25 (left); Hulton-Deutsch Collection/CORBIS/MAGMA, p. 23 (top); Phillips, The International Fine Art Auctioneers, U.K/ Bridgeman Art Library, p. 8 (bottom); INDEX/BRIDGEMAN ART LIBRARY, p. 8; North Wind Picture Archives, p.6 (bottom left), 13; Private Collection/Bridgeman Art Library, p. 24 (left); Courtesy of Wilma Morris and Joan Napier, daughters of William Gardiner, p. 19 (top, left); Maximilion Stock Ltd./Science Photo Library, p. 29, (top); Photo Researchers, p. 12, 23 (bottom)

Illustrations: Jim Chernishenko: p. 18; Dan Pressman: p. 16; David Wysotski; contents page, pp. 4-5

Cover: This golden statue is of the Goddess Isis, built to protect the shrine of the Egyptian Pharaoh Tutankhamen.

Title page: Gold jewelry is one of the most common uses of gold.

Published by
Crabtree Publishing Company

Copyright © **2004**

Cataloging-in-Publication Data

Edwards, Ron, 1947-
Gold / Ron Edwards & James Gladstone.
    p. cm. -- (Rocks, minerals, and resources)
  Includes index.
      ISBN 0-7787-1413-6 (rlb) -- ISBN 0-7787-1445-4 (pbk.)
  1. Gold--Juvenile literature. I. Gladstone, James, 1969- II. Title.
III. Series.
  TN420.E47 2004
  553.4'1--dc22
                                    2004000823
                                         LC

Contents

Golden treasure

Fear swept the crew as the dreaded flag bearing the skull and crossbones hove into view. Blackbeard, the most vicious pirate in the Caribbean, was about to attack the ship. He and his bloodthirsty men wanted gold. They would kill all aboard to get it.

The story of gold

The story of gold is an adventure involving kings, queens, pirates, explorers, conquerors, and the native peoples they conquered. Throughout history, gold has woven a magic spell over those it touched. Gold is beautiful and rare; a soft shiny metal that can be molded into many shapes. It has been used for money, jewelry, and to decorate special buildings such as palaces and places of worship. Wherever the precious metal was discovered, prospectors rushed to mine it, starting new cities and countries as they went. Gold and the people who love it have helped shape the world we live in today.

What is gold?

Gold is a mineral. A mineral is a natural substance, such as coal, stone, or rocks, that is usually found in the ground. Gold is inorganic, meaning that it is made up of materials that were never "alive." Gold is also considered a metal because it is shiny and is a good conductor of electricity.

In the crust

Gold is one of many elements, or substances that cannot be changed by normal **chemical** means, that are found in the Earth's **crust**. Gold has a warm, sunny color and because it does not react with air, water, and most **chemicals**, its shine never fades. In its natural state, gold is soft and easily shaped. When heated to 1,943° Fahrenheit (1,062° Celsius) it melts and can be poured into molds to form coins, gold bars, and other objects.

(above) Gold in its natural or "raw" state looks like chunks of rock.

(left) A golden image of the lion of San Marco from the 1400s. The lion is a symbol of the Italian city of Venice. Gold has signified wealth and power for thousands of years.

Spanish explorer-conqueror, or conquistador, Francisco Pizarro murdered and pillaged his way through Central and South America in his quest for gold. Here, Inca King Atahualpa kneels before Pizarro. Gold from the New World enriched the Spanish treasury.

Gold! Gold! Gold!

Stories have been told, movies made and legends born about the discovery of the world's great gold deposits. It is a saga of dreams, greed, ambition, and exploration. The first and greatest gold rush was in California in 1849. Some historians believe that only about 10,000 tons (10,161 tonnes) of gold were mined before then and that over 115,000 tons (116,845 tonnes) have been mined since.

Today, gold is mined around the world. There are major deposits in Canada, the southwestern United States, Russia, and South America. The most extensive gold mining operations are in South Africa and Zimbabwe.

Gold in history

Gold's rarity and beauty has given it value for thousands of years. Even the word gold sounds similar in many languages. For example, it is "gold" in English and German, "guld" in Danish, and "gulden" in Dutch.

Golden touch

According to legend, King Midas of Phyrgia, in what is now Greece, loved gold so much he asked the god Dionysius to give him the power to turn all he touched into gold. When this included his food and even his beloved daughter, a broken-hearted King Midas begged Dionysius to remove his "golden touch."

Unlike other metals, which were used by ancient peoples for tools and weapons, gold's main function was to be beautiful. Some historians believe that gold was the first metal people ever used. Lured by its shine, ancient people turned the soft metal into jewelry and decorative objects such as vases and drinking goblets. Some used it for money. The earliest gold coins were minted about 3,000 years ago in Turkey. By 550 B.C., Turkey's King Croesus had **amassed** a fortune. Five hundred years later, **Julius Caesar** used gold coins to pay his Roman legions, or army.

(right) The earliest gold coins were made in what is now Turkey.

The Egyptians

When English **archaeologist** Howard Carter, opened King Tutankhamen's tomb in 1927, he discovered a golden treasure. A mask of the young king's face was still bright and shiny after 3,000 years. The Egyptian kings, called pharaohs, believed gold was sacred. They covered themselves with gold jewelry and when they died, were buried with golden objects to use in the next world.

The discovery of King Tut's tomb by English archaeologist Howard Carter in 1927 touched off a new craze for ancient Egyptian artefacts, many of which were discovered as gleaming and golden as the day they were entombed.

Archaeologists discovered gold objects 3,000 years after they were buried in Egyptian pharaoh King Tut's tomb.

With gold in great demand, the pharaohs had to get it any way they could, including stealing it from their enemies. The Egyptians were among the earliest people to mine gold and the first to make maps of their gold mines. The mining was done by slaves and prisoners who worked in terrible conditions. They dug out the rock then ground the stone to a fine powder. Slaves added water and poured the mixture into square basins where the sediment was washed away. The gold remained in the basin and was collected.

The Romans

The **Roman Empire** existed about 2,000 years ago in what is now Italy. The Romans were very powerful. Their armies conquered much of the ancient world, bringing home slaves and prisoners who worked in, among other places, Roman gold mines. The Romans were great builders and engineers and invented new ways to mine gold. For above-ground mining, they diverted streams of water to mine **hydraulically** and built long chutes called sluices for carrying the rocks. The Romans also mined underground. To extract or remove the gold, they developed a method of "roasting" rocks. This meant heating the rock, washing it with cold water until it cracked and then picking the gold out from the fragments. After the Roman Empire fell in 476 A.D., gold became very scarce in Europe. A new source was needed but it would take almost 1,000 years before that source was found.

Few gold artefacts of the Inca and Aztec civilizations survived the Spanish conquest. Spanish conquistadors melted most of the gold plundered from them into gold bars.

El Dorado

When Christopher Columbus came to the New World in 1492, rich sources of gold opened up to European explorers. Legends and myths grew about a country called El Dorado, or "The Golden One," where explorers would fill the holds of their ships with the precious metal. Fueled by a desire for wealth, these adventurers set out to capture the new lands and, in the process, stole its peoples' gold and destroyed their **civilizations**.

(left) The Romans and other ancient peoples minted gold coins in order to make paying for items easier all over their empires.

Spanish conquistadors battle with the Inca for control over gold in their territories.

The Incas

Spanish greed for gold smashed the great Inca civilization in the part of South American that is now Peru, Colombia, and Chile. When the Spanish arrived in 1535, the powerful Incas had been ruling for over 200 years.

Sweat of the sun

The Incas treasured gold for its beauty. They called it "the sweat of the sun." The Incas did not mine gold but panned for it in streams. All their gold was crafted into jewelry and ceremonial objects. By law, all the gold and silver in the land belonged to the emperor and could not be removed from the capital city of Cuzco.

When the Spanish conquistador Francisco Pizarro, met with the Inca emperor, Atahualpa, he demanded a **ransom** of gold in exchange for Atahualpa's life. After receiving the ransom, Pizarro had Atahualpa strangled. The Spanish killed many Incas and their lust for gold destroyed the once great Inca empire.

The Aztecs

Spaniards seeking gold invaded the powerful Aztecs' civilization in 1519. The Aztecs lived in what is now Mexico and their capital, Tenochtitlán, was located where Mexico City stands today. Spanish conquistador Hernando Cortes landed in 1519 with 500 men. He took Montezuma, the Aztecs' emperor, as a hostage, stole Montezuma's gold objects, and shipped them back to Spain. By 1525, the Spaniards had fully conquered the Aztecs and destroyed their civilization. The remaining Aztecs were forced to work as slaves in gold mines and on Spanish estates.

Gold rushes

Gold in California! Eureka! The cry, from the Greek word meaning "I found it," flashed around the world, sending thousands of gold-seekers, racing to make their fortunes. The California gold rush of 1849 had begun.

The 49ers

When carpenter James Marshall found gold flakes in the American River near Sutter's Mill in Sacramento, he sparked a frenzy that attracted about 80,000 **prospectors** from all over the world. The 49ers, as they were called, came from as far away as Europe, China, and Australia to make their fortunes. Some found gold, others died or went home pennyless. The population swell turned the nearby port of San Francisco into a booming city and on September 9, 1850, California entered the Union as the 31st state.

Treasure seekers

Prospectors were daring treasure seekers. They came from around the world seeking their own El Dorado, or promise of riches.

Panning for gold

Placer gold is carried into rivers and streams from **lodes** or gold veins in rocks. To get the gold, a prospector put sand and gravel from the riverbed into a shallow pail or pan. The pan was held under water and swished back and forth so the gold, which is **denser** than water, sank to the bottom. The water washed away the sand, leaving the gold flakes and nuggets behind.

Early gold towns and camps were rough. People lived in wooden shacks with poor heat and no running water. Violence and lawlessness were major problems. Many people died from diseases that swept through the camps. An estimated 30 percent of the 49ers who raced to the California rush died of disease, accident, or violence.

Thousands of prospectors traveled over the difficult and dangerous Chilkoot Pass to get to the Klondike. Many others did not make it and turned back.

Gold in Australia!

Edward Hargraves, an unsuccessful 49er, noticed how similar the California gold fields and some parts of his native Australia were. In 1851, he struck gold at Ballarat in Central Victoria, Australia, setting off the Australian gold rush.

Gold in South Africa!

In 1886, South Africa became the scene of one of the biggest gold rushes of all time. In the other rushes, prospectors panned for gold. In South Africa the metal was mined because it was embedded in the rock. As a result, large **corporations** developed **complex** mining methods and modern gold mining was born. The new industry turned South Africa into a wealthy mining country.

Gold in the Yukon!

In 1896, George Carmack, an ex-sailor, was stunned when, instead of salmon, he pulled a gold nugget from the Klondike River. As the news spread, 100,000 prospectors rushed to the area on the border between Yukon Territory, Canada and Alaska. While some found gold, most were disappointed and many died of cold and exposure.

Prospectors struck claims or ownership of the section of land and stream they panned for gold.

Finding gold

Methods for finding gold have changed a lot since the early gold rushes. Modern prospectors are highly skilled experts who use their knowledge of landforms, rocks, and plants to locate new lodes to mine.

Where gold lies

Geologists, or scientists who study the Earth's structure, use many tools to find gold. They use topographic and geologic maps that show the landforms on the Earth's surface and below the ground. Geologists also test the land and soil to see if the rock found below the Earth's surface contains gold.

Placer and lode gold

Placer gold is gold that is embedded in rock. Over time, wind and rain wear away at the rock, exposing gold veins, or lodes. The wearing away, or abrasion, causes gold nuggets to break off, wash downhill and settle at the bottom of a stream or valley. Placer gold was the gold that prospectors panned for.

A miner in a South African gold mine cuts through rock to get to gold veins. He follows the spray painted lines on the rock that identify where to cut. South Africa has the world's most productive gold mines.

Native gold

Native or pure gold is sometimes found in placer deposits. Native gold is extremely rare, because most deposits are mixed with silver, iron, copper, or other metals. This mix is called an alloy.

Exploration and sampling

Geologists who search for gold fields also use aerial photographs to locate gold fields. After a site is found, geologists drill and sample the rock underground to determine its mineral content. If there is enough gold, mining can start.

Gold veins in rock are known as lode deposits. This vein runs through a chunk of rock crystal, or quartz.

Fool's gold

Prospectors called the shiny mineral iron pyrite "fool's gold" because they were fooled into thinking it was real. A glint of yellow in a rock often was, and still is, mistaken for gold. Unlike the real thing, however, iron pyrite is brittle and dissolves when heated. Inexperienced prospectors are sadly disappointed when they learn that their golden treasure is only a worthless rock.

Mining

People have been mining gold since ancient times, using shovels and buckets to cart rock out of the Earth. Thousands of years ago, the gold belonged to kings and pharoahs. Today, mining for gold is big business run by large mining companies.

Mining the ore

Gold deposits are usually found mixed with rock and other metals or elements. This mixture is called ore. When the gold is embedded in rock it is called a lode. To extract the gold from the rock, the ore has to be mined. There are two main ways to mine the ore: open pit and underground mining.

Scraping the surface

Open pit mining, or strip mining is used when the ore is located near the Earth's surface. Minors extract ore from shallow cuts made into the Earth. Machines with large shovels dig the ore and trucks take it from the mine to be processed.

A modern shaft mine

Underground gold mines are deep mazes of shafts and tunnels.

Miners blast rock in an underground shaft. The metal poles support the roof of the shaft and help prevent the rock from caving in.

Digging way down deep

Underground mining is used when ore is buried deep in the ground. For underground mining, miners dig, and mechanically blast long narrow passages, called shafts, down into the earth. They then dig and blast tunnels out from the shafts. Machines extract the ore and elevators bring it to the surface where trucks transport it from the mine.

At an open-pit mine, machines remove gold-laden ore nearer to the surface of the Earth.

Gold production

After the gold rush of the 1860s, South African miners abandoned placer gold and searched for lodes. They found them so far beneath the surface that some South African mines are as deep as 12,000 feet (3,700 meters). It would take over nine Empire State Buildings, at 1,250 feet (381 meters) tall stacked end to end to fill a 12,000-foot (3,700 meter) mineshaft. Today, South Africa mines and refines nearly 16 million troy ounces of gold each year.

Troy ounces

Troy ounces are a weight measurement used only for precious metals such as gold and silver. Named after a weight system developed in Troyes, France in the Middle Ages (500 to 1500 A.D.), one troy ounce equals about 1.1 ounces (31.1 grams). South Africa is the world's number one gold producer. The United States is second followed by Australia, Canada, and China.

World gold production

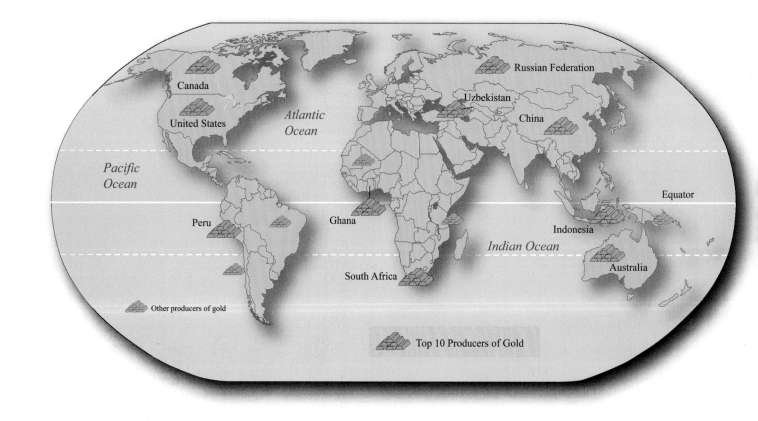

South Africa is the world's top gold producer. The United States is the second biggest gold producer.

Serial Number T-I0II5   Date of issue   OCT - 7 1969

Name of Holder   SUTHERLAND, John

Address

Mine No.

Country of Birth   Scotland

Date of Birth   I9I0-IV-29

Signature of Holder

FORM 44C   402-II5-836

I Certify that I have examined

John Sutherland

whose photograph is attached hereto, and that he is entitled to this Miner's Certificate.

Signature of Medical Officer.

RENEWAL OF MINER'S CERTIFICATE
To be completed by examiner.

TO BE RE-EXAMINED	DATE OF RE-EXAMINATION	SIGNATURE OF MEDICAL OFFICER RENEWING CERTIFICATE
OCT - 7 1970		

The medical officer will indicate in column 1 (above) the date before which holder should appear for re-examination.

In the past, many mining companies required miners to have identity permits, or mining cards. The cards included photographs taken during medical exams.

Children used to work transporting buckets of rock in gold mines because their size made it easier for them to work in tight spaces and because they could be paid less than adults. Child labor is now illegal in many parts of the world. These children are working today in a Bolivian gold mine.

Gold mining was, and still is, difficult and dangerous work. Miners worked in crews where they depended on each other for safety, and formed close relationships.

In constant danger

Like miners in the past, today's miners face many dangers. Explosions, rockslides, and flooding are some of the hazards they face. In recent years, mining companies started using earthquake detectors and huge air conditioners that keep the air in the mineshafts and tunnels safe for the miners to breathe and make their work more comfortable.

From ore to gold

Mining ore is only the first step in producing pure gold. The metal, which is often found mixed with silver, iron, or copper, is removed from rock and purified before it can be called gold. The separation and purification of gold from other metals is called refining.

Leaching

Leaching is the first step in turning ore into gold. After ore is mined, it is crushed into a powder, put into tanks, then mixed with air, chemicals, such as **cyanide**, and water. The air and cyanide dissolve the gold, and separate it from the ore.

Refining

Refining is the final step in producing pure gold. There are many ways to refine gold. One method is to "blow" the chemical chlorine through melted gold. The chlorine changes the other metals and makes them rise to the surface where they are removed. Electrolysis is a second method used to refine gold today. Gold is first extracted from ore using a solution of water and chemicals. An **electric current** is then passed through the solution and the gold, breaking the **bonds** that hold the gold and ore together.

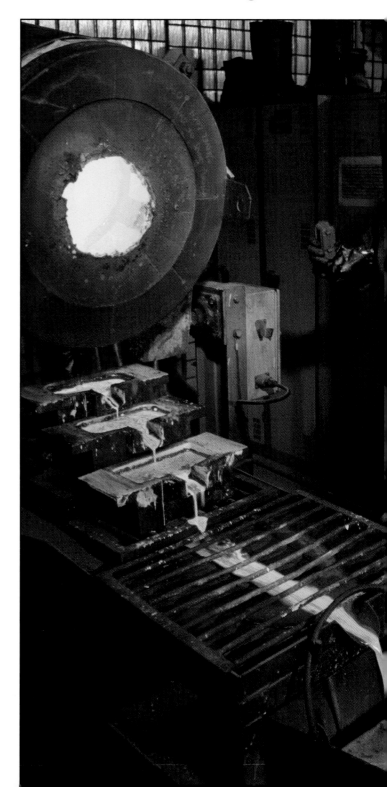

After the ore is ground into powder, it is leached to separate out the gold

Gold bars

Gold bars come in many sizes. The most common is a little smaller than a house brick. It weighs about 27 pounds (12.5 kg) and is 7 inches long, 3 1/2 inches wide, and 1 3/4 inches deep (20 cm long, 8 cm wide, and 4.5 cm deep).

Gold bars, no matter the size, are heavy because they contain so much gold. The most commonly made bar weighs 27 pounds (12.5 kg).

Refining gold in ancient times

Ancient peoples used gold unrefined, or as they found it. The gold was a mixture of copper, iron, or silver that they pulled out of crushed rock. Over time, they developed methods of separating gold from other metals.

Ancient Greeks used a process called cupellation to refine gold. They added lead to the ore, placed it in a container called a cupel and set it over a charcoal fire. With a **bellows** they used oxygen to create a chemical reaction that left the gold, often mixed with silver, behind. The gold and silver alloy was called white gold, or electrum. It was not until around 580 B.C., that a process was used to refine pure gold and separate gold from silver. Later, the Romans dissolved gold dust in **mercury**. The gold left behind in all three processes was melted down and cast into stone or clay molds.

Gold and the environment

When mining companies dig into the Earth searching for gold, they sometimes damage the environment and leave scars on the landscape.

Gold rushes scar the land

All over the world, whenever gold was found, prospectors rushed in to make their fortunes. Towns sprang up overnight and people destroyed forests as they chopped down trees to erect buildings. In their search for gold, miners **dammed** rivers. Many rivers were clogged with mud and gravel, killing fish and driving wildlife from the area.

The damage continues

Today's mines use big machines and chemicals to mine and refine gold. Chemicals such as mercury and cyanide are used to refine gold. The chemicals pollute the land and seep into water systems, where they kill plants and animals. People living near mines sometimes blame illnesses such as **lead poisoning**, cancer, and **birth defects** on the chemicals released in the mining operations.

Waste rock

Waste rock is the rock left over after gold is removed from ore. The rock is often treated with chemicals in the extraction process and later dumped in outdoor storage sites. Wind and rain wear down the rock, and the chemicals then seep out into the environment. The chemicals make their way into waterways, poisoning fish. Mining companies have been conducting studies to determine how to safely dispose of waste rock to lessen or eliminate its harmful effects.

(above) A hose drains the waste water from a refining operation into a tailings pond.

Reclaiming the land

There are three main reasons to reclaim land damaged by mining: public safety, protecting land and water from erosion and contamination, and returning the land to its pre-mining condition. To reclaim mined land, mining companies first seal all open mine shafts, then replace the soil and plant grass. For strip mines, this soil replacement is done in stages, as the mining in each section is completed. Plants and trees, usually native to the area, are replanted and the slopes covered with bales of straw to protect against water runoff. This process is called reforestation and revegetation. Unfortunately, in some areas of the world, environmental laws are slack and mines are not reclaimed at all.

The poisonous chemicals in waste rock pose a serious health and environmental threat.

Strip mining operations scar the landscape. In recent years, some mining companies have begun to fix the damage of the past and revegetate the lands where mines were located.

Gold and money

People have always needed money, in one form or another. Before money was invented, people traded goods for services and for other goods. This trading system was known as the barter system. In some parts of the world, bartering is still practiced today.

The beginning of money

Historians think the first coins were minted in 670 B.C. by King Gyges of Lydia, in present-day Turkey. These coins were made of the gold and silver alloy called electrum. In 550 B.C., Lydia's last king, Croesus minted coins that were 98 percent gold. Today, when people are very wealthy, we say they are as "rich as Croesus."

(below) In the past, bartering was used to trade goods among people from different cultures. In North America, European fur traders exchanged beads, blankets, and tools for furs trapped by Native hunters.

(left) The earliest coins were made from an alloy of silver and gold, called electrum.

Paper money did not become popular until the late 1600s.

Face value

Lydia's coins were the first to have a set value because they were minted from a precious metal, were all the same weight, and were guaranteed by the Lydian government. The coins introduced by King Croesus proved so successful that the concept quickly spread throughout Lydia's neighbor, Greece, and many other parts of the world.

Paper money

The word paper comes from papyrus, a reed-like plant whose inner core was stripped, soaked, and pressed into paper by the Egyptians. Paper made from tree bark was invented in China around 105 A.D. Paper money did not appear in China until around 700 A.D. Before then, people used other material to represent scrip, including leather, parchment, and clay tablets.

A papyrus illustration of how gold was melted down by workers in Ancient Egypt. Papyrus was a plant that was used to make paper.

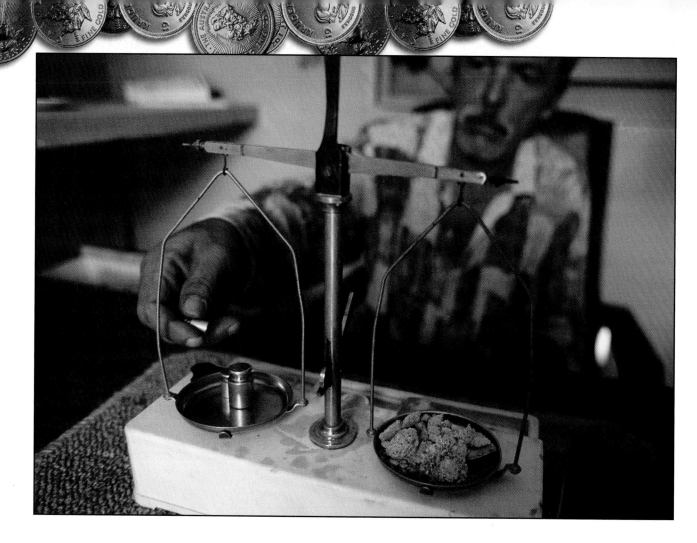

Paper for coin

In 1694, The Bank of England, which was then private, issued the first banknotes. Each note promised to pay a specified amount when **redeemed** at the bank. The next year the bank started using watermarked, or paper with water engraved design, notes to prevent people from counterfeiting, or printing their own banknotes.

(top) a gold buyer uses a scale to measure the weight of unprocessed gold. In some areas of the world, the value of gold jewelry is measured by weight.

In many countries gold jewelry is considered the best form of portable wealth because you can take it with you if you must leave a place quickly and you can sell it easily. These Afghani women are buying 24 karat gold jewelry in a market.

Fort Knox in Kentucky has been the main storage house for the United States' Government's gold reserves since 1937.

The gold standard

England introduced the gold standard in 1816, guaranteeing that each banknote was worth an exact amount of gold. The Bank of England, by then owned by the British government, stored its gold reserve in safes to guarantee a set value for the paper money. Other countries established similar gold reserves to back up their paper currency.

Karats

A karat is the weight used to measure the purity of gold. The word comes from units of mass, or weight, based on **carob seeds** used by merchants in the Middle East in ancient times. Since gold is soft, other metals such as silver or copper are often added to it to make it stronger. The word karat tells the buyer the amount of gold in an object. Six karats is 25 percent, 12 karats is 50 percent; 18 karats is 75 percent and 24 karats means pure gold.

Golden symbols

Gold has always had a magical effect on the people who see it, wear it, and desire it. Gold has been used for funeral masks for wealthy kings, rings that mark marriages, and even as a gleaming decoration for food.

Decorating with gold

Many religious and ornamental objects are decorated with gold leaf. Gold leaf is a thin foil or sheet made of gold. When applied to an object such as furniture, it is called gilt or gilding. Ormolu, or bronze or brass that has been gilded, is used to decorate furniture and other objects like urns and vases.

Illuminated manuscripts

In the Middle Ages, paper was scarce and very few people could write. Books were copied by hand by religious people who spent their lives carefully **transcribing** religious stories. Important religious works were decorated with gold leaf. This was very delicate work. These books were produced for the wealthy nobility and the **Catholic Church**.

Gold leaf, or gilding, has been used for thousands of years to decorate furniture, books, and other objects. This medieval manuscript has gold leaf lettering.

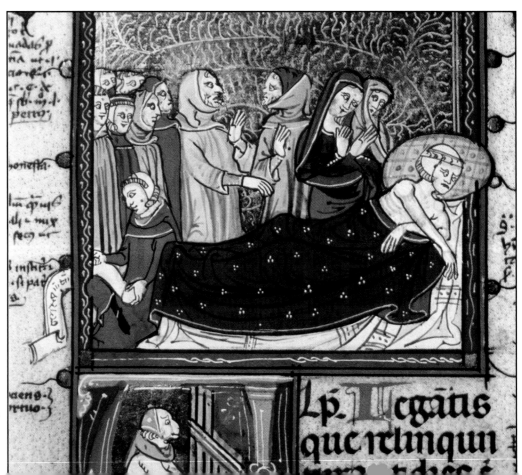

Factory workers produce gold foil to be used in stereo headphones. Gold is used in everything from dentistry to electronics.

Making jewelry

Crafting gold jewelry is a delicate art, traditionally done by hand. Gold is easily fashioned into intricate pieces, often in combination with precious and semi-precious stones. Craftspeople designed the jewelry, making it one piece at a time. At one time, gold was so expensive, only royalty or wealthy people wore it.

Mass production

Although many craftspeople still make jewelry by hand, today, most pieces are now mass produced. Once a ring, necklace, or other design is completed, it is manufactured in large quantities in a factory. Mass-produced jewelry is less expensive than that made by hand. In North America, 14 karat gold, mixed with copper, silver, and sometimes zinc, is the most common. It is hard and wears well. Europeans often favor the softer 18 karat gold.

Wedding in gold

In India, gold jewelry is part of the dowry or gift a bride brings to her new husband. For that reason, gold rings, chains, earrings, and bracelets are important parts of her bridal outfit. Gold is a portable dowry and can be easily sold if a family needs money. Indian gold jewelry is purchased by weight. Most Indian brides prefer 24 karat gold.

Gold in technology

Gold has uses today beyond jewelry and coins. Gold is used in making thermometers to take temperatures, in computer parts, and even in new medical treatments.

Gold in health

The ancient Egyptians used gold to fill decayed teeth because gold is easy to mold and does not corrode. Gold teeth used to be a sign of wealth, since the teeth of the poor were more likely to be rotting or missing. Today, dentists continue to use gold for fillings and crowns, but material that looks natural is more popular. Gold is now used as a material in laser eye surgery and surgeons have long used gold instruments in delicate surgeries such as heart surgery. Gold is also now being used to treat some illnesses such as **rheumatoid arthritis**. Researchers believe that gold, taken in pill form, reduces swelling and pain caused by the disease.

Gold film reflects the heat of the sun, keeping the inside of buildings cool on hot summer days. In bright sunlight, the reflecting windows glow like candle flames. Gold's excellent conductivity makes it important to the electrical and electronics industries.

Gold in technology

Many of the properties that made gold popular for decoration have now turned it into a valuable substance for modern technology. When some metals mix with oxygen, they oxidize or corrode and can no longer conduct electricity. Gold does not oxidize, so it is widely used in the electrical and electronics industries in circuit boards and other communications tools.

One interesting use of gold is in Air Force One, the plane used by the president of the United States. Air Force One has gold plated reflectors that, in the event of an enemy attack, confuse a missile's heat-seaking guidance system. Gold reflects the heat, making the missile miss its target.

Modern scientists extract gold from rock with the help of chemicals and machinery.

Alchemy

Gold was so valued thousands of years ago that people called alchemists tried to make it from other minerals and plants. Along the way they found other useful substances such as acids and barium sulfide, a material that glows in the dark. Alchemists never made gold and alchemy died out but their methods helped establish the science of chemistry.

Glossary

amassed Gathered together for profit

archaeologist A person who studies cultures of the past

bellows A device that produces a strong blast of air

birth defects Abnormalities children are born with

bonds Uniting or binding forces

Catholic Church Christian church with the Pope in Rome as its head

carob seeds watermelon seed sized seeds from the pod of a tree.

chemicals Substances used in industry

civilizations The way of life of a group of people in history

corporations Businesses or big organizations

complex Something that is difficult

crust The outermost layer of the Earth

cyanide A poisonous chemical

dam A barrier across a waterway that controls the flow

denser Packed more closely together

electric current An energy current or flow

hydraulically Machinery operated by a fluid, especially water

Julius Caesar A Roman emperor, or leader who ruled, expanded Rome's territory, and his empire, and lived from 100 to 44 B.C

Latin The language of ancient Rome

lead poisoning Poisoning caused by the metal lead

lodes Gold embedded in rock

mercury A silvery-white poisonous metalic element

processed Prepared for final use

prospectors People who explore for gold

ransom Money demanded so that a person held prisoner can go free

redeemed Cashed in

rheumatoid arthritis A disease that makes people stiff and sore in the joints

Roman Empire An ancient empire, ruled by Romans that lasted from 27 B.C. to 410 A.D. and extended from Egypt to England at its most powerful

treasury A place where money is kept

Index

1 2 3 4 5 6 7 8 9 0   Printed in the USA   0 9 8 7 6 5 4 3 2 1